A Common Prayer

Leunig

He that shuts Love out, in turn shall be
Shut out from Love, and on her threshold lie
Howling in the outer darkness.

Tennyson

Love is like bread. It has to be made fresh every day.

Old Saying

Love is the bright foreigner, the foreign self.

Emerson

CollinsDove
A Division of HarperCollins*Publishers*

Published by Collins Dove
A Division of HarperCollins*Publishers* (Australia) Pty Ltd
22-24 Joseph Street
North Blackburn, Victoria 3130

First published 1990, reprinted 1990, 1991 (four times), 1992 (twice), 1993
Designed by John Canty
Cover design by John Canty
Cover illustration by Michael Leunig

Typeset in 12/20 Bodoni by Southern Cross Typesetting
Printed in Australia by McPherson's Printing Group

The National Library of Australia
Cataloguing-in-Publication Data:

Leunig, Michael, 1945-
A common prayer.

ISBN 0 85924 933 6
1. Prayers. I. Title.

242

ACKNOWLEDGEMENTS

The ideas and the spirit of this book have arisen from a difficult personal situation of upheaval and change and from the vital inspiration and support I received from a number of people during that time.

In particular I acknowledge with gratitude the care, the commitment and the insightful work of Anne Clancy; the gentleness and courage of my children, Gus Leunig and Sunny Leunig; and the comradeship and loving presence of Helga Salwe.

PREFACE

The prayers contained in this book were created for publication in Melbourne's *Sunday Age* newspaper. Their publication was something of a small experiment both for myself, when I decided to create them, and for the editor of the *Sunday Age*, Steve Harris, who supported the idea and published them without reservation.

I was originally asked to draw a weekly cartoon for the paper but I found it difficult to be enthused. I felt there were already enough jokes and amusements at hand and the boom in humour and satire I found somewhat oppressive.

It seemed to me that newspapers might carry some small spiritual message of consolation as a tiny reparation for the enormous anxiety and distress I believe they can create, an anxiety and distress which I felt was not and could not be addressed or relieved by humorists.

Prayer as a creative lacuna, as an ancient free form and as a marvellous, stabilising idea, intrigued me greatly.

The spirit of the times, so constricted by fashion anxiety, so repressed by ego and scientific authority, seemed the ideal climate for the cultivation of public prayers.

The presence of any sincere prayer (and as Mark Twain observed, 'You can't pray a lie') in the realm of contemporary journalism was likely to create a small, embarrassing and healthy juxtaposition, and knowing that such juxtapositions must *always* be attempted, I set out awkwardly to write prayers for the newspaper. All I hoped was that my efforts might help revitalise the *idea* of prayer.

I also wanted to gently foster the notion that the mass media might take on a spiritual responsibility. I learned much as I proceeded.

The nature and the words of the particular prayers in this book are perhaps not as important as the idea of prayer itself. After all, these are public prayers, which makes them seem a bit impersonal and contrived. Some of them are expressions of hope, some are declarations, others are thanksgivings. Their creation has involved feelings of considerable vulnerability, because I understand that such things are readily and gladly misunderstood. They are my fumbling experiments and they mostly derive from a deep and difficult personal struggle.

The book, however, is offered as something of a prayer itself. I hope it somehow contributes to the illumination of this small, ancient, wonderful, free-form, do-it-yourself ritual of connection, love and transformation, the common prayer.

INTRODUCTION

I have drawn a simple picture of a person kneeling before a duck to symbolise and demonstrate my ideas and feelings about the nature of prayer. I ask the reader to bear with the absurdity of the image and to remember that the search for the sublime may sometimes have a ridiculous beginning. Here then is the story behind the picture.

A man kneels before a duck in a sincere attempt to talk with it. This is a clear depiction of irrational behaviour and an important aspect of prayer. Let us put this aside for the moment and move on to the particulars.

The act of kneeling in the picture symbolises humility. The upright stance has been abandoned because of the human attitudes and qualities it represents: power, stature, control, rationality, worldliness, pride and ego. The kneeling man knows, as everybody does, that a proud and upright man does not and cannot talk with a duck. So the upright stance is rejected. The man kneels. He humbles himself. He comes closer to the duck. He becomes more like the duck. He does these things because it improves his chances of communicating with it.

The duck in the picture symbolises one thing and many things: nature, instinct, feeling, beauty, innocence, the primal, the non-rational and the mysterious unsayable; qualities we can easily attribute to a duck and qualities which, coincidentally and remarkably, we can easily attribute to the inner life of the kneeling man, to his spirit or his soul. The duck then, in this picture, can be seen as a symbol of the human spirit, and in wanting connection with his spirit it is a symbolic picture of a man searching for his soul.

The person cannot actually see this 'soul' as he sees the duck in the picture but he can feel its enormous impact on his life. Its outward manifestations can be disturbing and dramatic and its inner presence is often wild and rebellious or elusive and difficult to grasp: but the person knows that from this inner dimension, with all its turmoil, comes his love and his fear, his creative spark, his music, his art and his very will to live. He also feels that a strong relationship with this inner world seems to lead to a good relationship with the world around him and a better life. Conversely, he feels that alienation from these qualities, or loss of spirit, seems to cause great misery and loneliness.

He believes in this spiritual dimension, this inner life, and he knows that it can be strengthened by acknowledgement and by giving it a name.

He may call it the human spirit, he may call it the soul or he may call it god. The particular name is not so very important.

The point is that he acknowledges this spiritual dimension. He would be a fool to ignore it, so powerful is its effect on his life so joyous, so mysterious, so frightening.

Not only does he recognise and name it but he is intensely curious about it. He wants to explore it and familiarise himself with its ways and its depth. He wants a robust relationship with it, he wants to trust it, he wants its advice and the vitality it provides. He also wants to feed it, this inner world, to care for it and make it strong. It's important to him.

And the more he does these things, this coming to terms with his soul, the more his life takes on a sense of meaning. The search for the spirit leads to love and a better world, for him and for those around him. This personal act is also a social and political act because it affects so many people who may be connected to the searcher.

But how do we search for our soul, our god, our inner voice? How do we find this treasure hidden in our life? How do we connect to this transforming and healing power? It seems as difficult as talking to a bird. How indeed?

There are many ways, all of them involving great struggle, and each person must find his or her own way. The search and the relationship is a lifetime's work and there is much help available, but an important, perhaps essential part of this process seems to involve an ongoing, humble acknowledgement of the soul's existence and integrity. Not just an intellectual recognition but also a ritualistic, perhaps poetic, gesture of acknowledgement: a respectful tribute.

Why it should need to be like this is mysterious, but a ceremonial affirmation, no matter how small, seems to carry an indelible and resonant quality into the heart which the intellect is incapable of carrying.

Shaking the hand of a friend is such a ritual. It reaffirms something deep and unsayable in the relationship. A non-rational ritual acknowledges and reaffirms a non-rational, but important, part of the relationship. It is a small but vital thing.

This ritual of recognition and connection is repeatable and each time it occurs something important is revitalised and strengthened. The garden is watered.

And so it is with the little ritual which recognises the inner life and attempts to connect to it. This do-it-yourself ceremony where the mind is on its knees; the small ceremony of words which calls on the soul to come forth. This ritual known simply as prayer.

The garden is watered.

A person kneels before a duck and speaks to it with sincerity. The person is praying.

Christmas.

Dear God, it is timely that we give thanks for the lives of all prophets, teachers, healers and revolutionaries, living and dead, acclaimed or obscure, who have rebelled, worked and suffered for the cause of love and joy.

We also celebrate that part of us, that part within ourselves, which has rebelled, worked and suffered for the cause of love and joy.

We give thanks and celebrate.

Amen.

God help us to change. To change ourselves and to change our world. To know the need for it. To deal with the pain of it. To feel the joy of it. To undertake the journey without understanding the destination. The art of gentle revolution.

Amen.

God give us strength. Strength to hold on and strength to let go.
Amen.

That which is Christ-like within us shall be crucified. It shall suffer and be broken. And that which is Christ-like within us shall rise up. It shall love and create.

Dear God,

We give thanks for the darkness of the night where lies the world of dreams. Guide us closer to our dreams so that we may be nourished by them. Give us good dreams and memory of them so that we may carry their poetry and mystery into our daily lives.

Grant us deep and restful sleep that we may wake refreshed with strength enough to renew a world grown tired.

We give thanks for the inspiration of stars, the dignity of the moon and the lullabies of crickets and frogs.

Let us restore the night and reclaim it as a sanctuary of peace, where silence shall be music to our hearts and darkness shall throw light upon our souls. Good night.

Sweet dreams.

Amen.

God give us rain when we expect sun.
Give us music when we expect trouble.
Give us tears when we expect breakfast.
Give us dreams when we expect a storm.
Give us a stray dog when we expect
congratulations.
God play with us, turn us sideways and
around.
Amen.

Dear God,

We give thanks for birds. All types of birds. Small birds and large birds. Domestic fowls, migratory birds and birds of prey, hooting birds, whistling birds, shrikes, colored parrots and dark darting wrens. Birds too numerous to mention. We praise them all.

We mourn the loss of certain species and pray for the deliverance of endangered ones. We pray, too, for farm birds, that they may be released from cruelty and suffering.

We give thanks for eggs and feathers, for brave, cheerful songs in the morning and the wonderful, haunting, night prayers of owls, mopokes, frogmouths and all nocturnal fowls.

We praise the character of birds, their constancy, their desire for freedom, their flair for music and talent for flying. May we always marvel at their ability to fly. Especially we praise their disregard for the human hierarchy and the ease with which they leave their droppings on the heads of commoners or kings regardless. Grant them fair weather, fresh food and abundant materials for building their nests in spring. Provide them too with perches and roosts with pleasant aspects. Dear God, guide our thoughts to the joy and beauty of birds. Feathered angels. May they always be above us.

Amen.

Dear God,

Give comfort and peace to those who are separated from loved ones. May the ache in their hearts be the strengthening of their hearts. May their longing bring resolve to their lives, conviction and purity to their love. Teach them to embrace their sadness lest it turn to despair. Transform their yearning into wisdom. Let their hearts grow fonder.

Amen.

There are only two feelings. Love and fear.
There are only two languages. Love and fear.
There are only two activities. Love and fear.
There are only two motives, two procedures,
two frameworks, two results. Love and fear.
Love and fear.

Dear God,

These circumstances will change. This situation shall pass.

Amen.

God bless the lost, the confused, the unsure, the bewildered, the puzzled, the mystified, the baffled, and the perplexed.

Amen.

It is time to plant tomatoes. Dear God, we praise this fruit and give thanks for its life and evolution. We salute the tomato, cheery, fragrant morsel, beloved provider, survivor and thriver and giver of life. Giving and giving and giving. Plump with summer's joy. The scent of its stem is summer's joy, is promise and rapture. Its branches breathe perfume of promise and rapture. Giving and giving and giving.

Dear God, give strength to the wings and knees of pollinating bees, give protection from hailstorms, gales and frosts, give warm days and quenching rains. Refresh and adorn our gardens and our tables. Refresh us with tomatoes.

Rejoice and rejoice! Celebrate the scarlet soul of winter sauces. Behold the delicious flavor! Behold the oiled vermilion moons that ride and dive in olive-bobbing seas of vinegared lettuce. Let us rejoice! Let this rejoicing be our thanks for tomatoes.

Amen.

Dear God,

Let us prepare for winter. The sun has turned away from us and the nest of summer hangs broken in a tree. Life slips through our fingers and, as darkness gathers, our hands grow cold. It is time to go inside. It is time for reflection and resonance. It is time for contemplation. Let us go inside. Amen.

Let us pray for wisdom. Let us pause from thinking and empty our mind. Let us stop the noise. In the silence let us listen to our heart. The heart which is buried alive. Let us be still and wait and listen carefully. A sound from the deep, from below. A faint cry. A weak tapping. Distant muffled feelings from within. The cry for help.

We shall rescue the entombed heart. We shall bring it to the surface, to the light and the air. We shall nurse it and listen respectfully to its story. The heart's story of pain and suffocation, of darkness and yearning. We shall help our feelings to live in the sun. Together again we shall find relief and joy.

Dear God,

We struggle, we grow weary, we grow tired. We are exhausted, we are distressed, we despair. We give up, we fall down, we let go. We cry. We are empty, we grow calm, we are ready. We wait quietly.

A small, shy truth arrives. Arrives from without and within. Arrives and is born. Simple, steady, clear. Like a mirror, like a bell, like a flame. Like rain in summer. A precious truth arrives and is born within us. Within our emptiness.

We accept it, we observe it, we absorb it. We surrender to our bare truth. We are nourished, we are changed. We are blessed. We rise up.

For this we give thanks.

Amen.

Dear God,

We pray for balance and exchange. Balance us like trees. As the roots of a tree shall equal its branches so must the inner life be equal to the outer life. And as the leaves shall nourish the roots so shall the roots give nourishment to the leaves. Without equality and exchange of nourishment there can be no growth and no love.
Amen.

Dear God,

We give thanks for places of simplicity and peace. Let us find such a place within ourselves. We give thanks for places of refuge and beauty. Let us find such a place within ourselves. We give thanks for places of nature's truth and freedom, of joy, inspiration and renewal, places where all creatures may find acceptance and belonging. Let us search for these places: in the world, in ourselves and in others. Let us restore them. Let us strengthen and protect them and let us create them.

May we mend this outer world according to the truth of our inner life and may our souls be shaped and nourished by nature's eternal wisdom.

Amen.

God be with the mother. As she carried her child may she carry her soul. As her child was born, may she give birth and life and form to her own, higher truth. As she nourished and protected her child, may she nourish and protect her inner life and her independence. For her soul shall be her most painful birth, her most difficult child and the dearest sister to her other children. Amen.

God help us. With great skill and energy we have ignored the state of the human heart. With politics and economics we have denied the heart's needs. With eloquence, wit and reason we have belittled the heart's wisdom. With sophistication and style, with science and technology, we have drowned out the voice of the soul. The primitive voice, the innocent voice. The truth. We cannot hear our heart's truth and thus we have betrayed and belittled ourselves and pledged madness to our children. With skill and pride we have made for ourselves an unhappy society. God be with us.
Amen.

God be amongst us and within us. Earth is our mother and nature's law is our father, our protector. Thus, we pray.

Father do not forgive them for they know precisely what they do. Those destroyers of earth's beauty and goodness, those killers of nature, do not forgive them.

Those betrayers of nature's love.
Those exploiters of nature's innocence.
Those poisoners. Do not forgive them.

Those greedy, pompous people. That greed and pomposity within us all. The sum total of that petty greed and pomposity within us all. We now know precisely what these things are doing to this earth. So Father, do not forgive us for we now understand what it is that we do.
Amen.

We pray for the fragile ecology of the heart and the mind. The sense of meaning. So finely assembled and balanced and so easily overturned. The careful, ongoing construction of love. As painful and exhausting as the struggle for truth and as easily abandoned.

Hard fought and won are the shifting sands of this sacred ground, this ecology. Easy to desecrate and difficult to defend, this vulnerable joy, this exposed faith, this precious order. This sanity.

We shall be careful. With others and with ourselves.

Amen.

Dear God,

We celebrate spring's returning and the rejuvenation of the natural world. Let us be moved by this vast and gentle insistence that goodness shall return, that warmth and life shall succeed, and help us to understand our place within this miracle. Let us see that as a bird now builds its nest, bravely, with bits and pieces, so we must build human faith. It is our simple duty; it is the highest art; it is our natural and vital role within the miracle of spring: the creation of faith.

Amen.

God accept our prayers.

Send us tears in return.

Give freedom to this exchange.

Let us pray inwardly.

Let us weep outwardly.

This is the breathing of the soul.

This is the vitality of the spirit.

For this we give thanks.

Amen.

Dear God,

When we fall, let us fall inwards. Let us fall freely and completely: that we may find our depth and humility: the solid earth from which we may rise up and love again.

Amen.

Dear God,

We loosen our grip.
We open our hand.
We are accepting.
In our empty hand
We feel the shape
Of simple eternity.
It nestles there.
We hold it gently.
We are accepting.
Amen.

We give thanks for domestic animals. Those creatures who can trust us enough to come close. Those creatures who can trust us enough to be true to themselves.

They approach us from the wild. They approach us from the inner world. They bring beauty and joy, comfort and peace.

For this miracle and for the lesson of this miracle. We give thanks.

Amen.

The path to your door
Is the path within:
Is made by animals,
Is lined by flowers,
Is lined by thorns,
Is stained with wine,
Is lit by the lamp of sorrowful dreams:
Is washed with joy,
Is swept by grief,
Is blessed by the lonely traffic of art:
Is known by heart,
Is known by prayer,
Is lost and found,
Is always strange,
The path to your door.

'Love one another and you will be happy.'
It's as simple and as difficult as that. There is no other way.
Amen.